# THE
# MAGIC OF POETRY
# AND
# THE POET'S ART

*by*

*Stephen Vincent Benét*

# Stephen Vincent Benét

Stephen Vincent Benét was born on 22nd July 1898 in Bethlehem, Pennsylvania, United States.

Benét was sent to the Hitchcock Military Academy at the age of ten and then continued his education at The Albany Academy in New York. He also attended Yale University where he received his M.A. in English.

Benét was an accomplished writer at an early age, having had his first book published at 17 and submitting his third volume of poetry in lieu of a thesis for his degree. During his time at Yale, he was an influential figure at the 'Yale Lit' literary magazine, and a fellow member of the Elizabethan Club. Benét was also a part-time contributor for the early Time Magazine.

Benét's involvement with the University literary scene led to a decade-long judgeship of the Yale Series of Younger Poets Competition. He is also responsible for publishing the first volumes of work by authors such as James Agee, Muriel Rukeyser, Jeremy Ingalls, and Margaret Walker. In 1931, he was elected as a fellow of the American Academy of Arts ad Sciences.

Benét's best known works are the book-length narrative poem *American Civil War, John Brown's Body* (1928), for which he won a Pulitzer Prize in 1929, and two short stories, *The Devil and Daniel Webster* (1936) and *By the Waters of Babylon* (1937). Benét won a second Pulitzer Prize posthumously for his unfinished poem *Western Star* in 1944.

Stephen Vincent Benét died of a heart attack in New York City, on 13th March, 1943, and is buried in Evergreen Cemetery, Stonington, Conneticut.

# FOREWORD

MOST *small children love rhythm, yet many boys and girls reach maturity without a real appreciation of poetry.*

*For years the editors of Compton's have wanted an article for the encyclopedia which would help to bridge the gap between this instinctive liking for musical cadence and a true understanding of poetry. To find just the person to write the article was not easy. Many men have written poems. Few poets have tried to put into words their feeling for poetry. Almost none have attempted to tell the story of their art in a way to interest boys and girls. Anne Carroll Moore said, "Stephen Vincent Benét could do it." And so he could—and so he did.*

*The new article by Mr. Benét is included in the nineteenth edition of Compton's Pictured Encyclopedia. Because we like his interpretation of poetry so well, we have reprinted it in this booklet as our contribution to the Fifty-Seventh Conference of the American Library Association, Richmond, Virginia, May 11-16, 1936.*

# ACKNOWLEDGMENTS

*The publishers wish to express grateful apprecia-
tion for permission to use the following copyrighted
material:*

To Henry Holt and Company for "The Cherry Tree",
in 'A Shropshire Lad', by A. E. Housman

To Houghton Mifflin Company for "The Sonnet", by
Richard Watson Gilder

To Doubleday, Doran and Company for "As toilsome
I wandered Virginia's woods", in 'Leaves of Grass',
by Walt Whitman

To Farrar and Rinehart for "When Daniel Boone goes
by" in 'A Book of Americans', "I have fallen in love
with American names" in 'Ballads and Poems', and
other quotations from the poetry of Stephen Vincent
Benét

F. E. COMPTON

# THE MAGIC OF POETRY

## AND

## THE POET'S ART

*How the Music of Verse Is Made
by Rhyme, Meter, and Pattern*

POETRY is one of the oldest of the arts and one of the most persistent. We do not know who the first person was who had the idea of telling a story or expressing a thought in rhythmic, chanting words with a strong and easily remembered beat. Perhaps he thudded a drum-log by some very early campfire and, as he thought of his day's hunting or the fearfulness of the night or his own bravery, began to fit words to the rough tune. He would chant and stamp and beat as he made those words. Where the words did not fill out the tune, he would give a shout or a cry. That must have been the earliest and most primitive form of poetry—rhythmic words, chanted aloud to a rough musical accompaniment or to no accompaniment at all but the stamp of the chanter's feet on the ground, the slap of his hands on his body to mark the pulse of the song.

He was saying something, but he was singing it as well; he was making his words a drum-beat or the rush of a storm, a prayer or a call to battle. If he had merely wanted to tell his friends that he was hungry or that he had seen a fine herd of deer in the forest, he would not have needed the drum or the cry or the chant. He would have said what he had to say in prose, as we do when we write an ordinary letter about ordinary things. But he wanted to do more than that. He wanted his friends to remember what he said and to think about it. He wanted to excite and stir them as he was excited and stirred. So he made a song, in words.

Then, if people liked the song, they would listen. A very famous song might be passed down and down through the generations by word of mouth, until there got to be something sacred about it. Till, at last, poems were written down—and Alexander the Great, as he strove to conquer the world, carried Homer's 'Iliad' about with him in a gold casket; and James Wolfe, the great British general, told his council, on the eve of victory, that he would rather have written Gray's 'Elegy' than capture Quebec. For that is the way that great men and great nations have felt about great poetry. They have thought of it not as a task or an ornament, but as an essential part of the greatness of life.

### THE POET'S PURPOSE

It is a long way from the chanting singer, in the red light of the campfire, to the printed book of verse in your library. But the road is a clear one, and the poet's intent the same. He is trying to tell you something—perhaps a story about gods or heroes, about lumberjacks or sailors or the people you meet every day—perhaps merely about his own feelings when he sees a cloud or a flower—perhaps about the mysterious things of life, the things like death and birth and the great empty places between the stars which make us feel small and wondering when we stand before them. But he is trying to tell it to you rhythmically, in musical words that will stir your imagination and leave a magic pattern on your mind. Most people talk a great deal but say very little; the poet tries to talk very little but say a great deal. He wants to make you see what he has seen and feel what he has felt. To do so, he uses words not only for their meaning but for their ring and music —as a composer uses the sound of certain musical instruments, alone or in combination, when he wishes to make you think of the sea or the forest, of the trumpets of battle or the voices of lovers at night.

### THE MUSIC IN PRIMITIVE POETRY

We know what primitive poetry is like; we have very fine examples of it in the ceremonial chants of our own North American Indians. When the Indian singer chants, in his own language, to the drum-beat

> The corn grows by the red rock.
> Beautifully it grows

he could hardly make a plainer or more simple song. In the English translation we miss the drum-beat, we miss the music of the Indian words for corn and rock and the rest. But we notice this: In the first place, the singer has seen something beautiful, something he wishes to share with his fellows. To do so, he does not merely make a direct statement, "I saw six fine ears of corn growing by a red rock." He repeats words for their sound, he arranges a musical pattern of words to fit his idea. So we get the beginnings of poetry.

When we reach a slightly more civilized form of poetry—the poetry of the ballads of the Scottish Border, for instance—we still hear the musical accompaniment with the words:

> Ye Hielands and ye Lowlands,
> O where hae ye been?
> They hae slain the Earl of Murray
> And laid him on the green.

We can hear the harper harping the notes and the voice singing. Indeed, this poem has been set to music many times. But the music is in the words as well. Rearrange the words in another way: "Where have you been, Highlands and Lowlands? His enemies have killed the Earl of Murray and laid him on the greensward." The sense is the same, but most of the music has gone. And, with the music, has gone another quality, that of intensity. The first passage, somehow, is not only more musical but more exciting than the second. And intensity, excitement, a keying-up of the mind as the body is keyed to a sudden spurt in a race, is one of the qualities of poetry.

Poetry is beat and rhythm and dance. It does not walk. It runs, skips, soars, flies. It can move as massively as a great ship down the launching-ways; it can move as delicately and subtly as the wind through a field of grass.

> When Ajax strives some rock's vast weight to throw,
> The line, too, labours, and the words move slow.

And when

High on a throne of royal state, which far
Outshone the wealth of Ormus and of Ind . . .
Satan exalted sate, . . .

the rich, slow, ponderous words build up the portentous
majesty of that evil throne. But when

All the girls are out with their baskets for the primrose;
Up lanes, woods through, they troop in joyful bands.—

the whole verse sparkles and dances. You could not say
it slowly and gloomily if you wished. There is in it the
light-footed hurry of a joyful throng.

It is natural that it should be so. For poetry is pri-
marily a rhythmic thing. In books, as in all writing, it
consists of words printed on a page. But these words
are meant to be heard with the ear as well as read by
the eye. Unless you can find and listen to the rhythm
of the words of a poem, you are missing half the poem.

How is poetry written? How "out of five sounds"
does the poet make "not a sixth sound but a star"?
Each language and each literature has its own ways.
Greek poetry, for instance, was based not upon rhyme
but upon beat—upon the beat of certain meters (line
lengths), like the surge of waves on a beach—and the
ebb and flow of syllables in the individual lines which
gave variation to the master beat. English poetry has
been strongly rhyming, although it has employed many
unrhymed forms, notably blank verse and free verse
(*vers libre*). Each poetry has developed certain rules,
certain forms or molds, certain meters which seemed
to bring out the most musical and imaginative qualities
of its own language.

Certain forms die, are revived, and die again. Certain ways of writing poetry are employed by one age, scorned by another, reworked perhaps by a third. Cultivated Frenchmen of the Eighteenth Century, used to the stately classicism of Corneille and Racine, found Shakespeare's work crude, barbarous, and violent. They thought of him as some of our own conventional critics thought of Walt Whitman—the sort of person you shouldn't let into your house because he might wipe his muddy feet on your best carpets. On the other hand, to many of us who are used to English poetry, reading Corneille and Racine is rather like wandering through a vast marble colonnade. We know that it is great, but we miss, in its cool perfection, the warmth, the intimacy, and the color of our own verse. And it is so even among works in the same language. You may like one sort of poetry very much and dislike another extremely. You may, for instance, think 'Paradise Lost' a dull and tedious affair and 'The Highwayman' an exciting adventure. But, before you shut any kind of poetry out of your mind, it is a good thing to see what the poet has tried to do and what sort of tools he has used to build his poem.

A poem must be imaginative enough to stir your own imagination. That is its first necessity; and if it does not do that to you as a reader, it is not a poem for you. It may be a very good poem to another reader whose mind, so to speak, tunes in on a different wavelength from yours—but that is another matter.

What tools does the poet use to make his rhythmic pattern, the pattern with which he hopes to stir your imagination? He has three chief tools—rhyme, meter, and pattern. He uses them in various combinations.

## RHYME

Let us start with the simplest tool, the one most familiar to us—rhyme. What is a rhyme? A rhyme is a pair of words which end with the same sound but begin differently.

> Hickory dickory dock.
> The mouse ran up the clock.

*Dock* and *clock* are rhymes. So are *Mary* and *contrary*, *Horner* and *corner*, *pail*, *whale*, and *sail*, and thousands more. But *soar* and *sore* are not rhymes. They are spelled differently, but the sound is identical; both the beginning- and end-sounds are the same.

In words of more than one syllable, the rhyme must be where the emphasis is. Thus *ailing* and *failing* are rhymes, because the emphasis on each word is on *ail* and *fail*. But *ailing* and *thing* are not true rhymes, as the emphasis in *ailing* is on the *ail* sound and the emphasis in *thing* is on the *ing* sound. Rhymes, in general, should rhyme to the ear, not to the eye, although in English there is a certain limited class of words that rhyme to the eye and not to the ear—*wind* (as we now pronounce it) and *blind,* for example, or *loving* and *roving*—which usage has made allowable.

And, in modern poetry, particularly, you will find a great deal of assonance—of words like *shadow* and *meadow* with similar but not identical sounds.

> Suppose, when you're lonely,
>     There's nought in your kettles
> But bread broken stonily
>     And serpentish victuals

says Elinor Wylie, in her beautiful 'Grace Before Meat'. Here all four rhymes are assonantal.

But in general the person who is beginning to write poetry—not the expert—should try to make his rhymes as clear and true as possible, if he writes in rhymed form. For rhymes are the bells of English verse, and there are rhymes of every sound and every metal. You can set a whole peal ringing at once, as Poe did in 'The Bells' or as Southey did in 'How the Waters Come Down at Lodore':

> Advancing and prancing and glancing and dancing . . .
> And dashing and flashing and splashing and clashing.

You can ring them against each other, single rhymes against double rhymes:

> So, we'll go no more a roving,
>   So late into the night,
> Though the heart be still as loving
>   And the moon be still as bright.

You can play tricks with them, as W. S. Gilbert did in his patter songs:

> From the greengrocer tree you get grapes and green pea, cauli-
> flowers, pineapple and cranberries,
> While the pastry-cook plant, cherry-brandy will grant, apple
> puffs and three corners and banberries.

You can use very simple rhymes, as A. E. Housman does in his perfect

> Loveliest of trees, the cherry now
> Is hung with bloom along the bough,
> And stands about the woodland ride
> Wearing white for Eastertide.
>
> Now, of my three score years and ten,
> Twenty will not come again,
> And take from seventy springs a score,
> It only leaves me fifty more.

And since to look at things in bloom
Fifty springs are little room,
About the woodlands I will go
To see the cherry hung with snow.

You can use rather odd ones, as Browning often does:

I the Trinity illustrate
Drinking watered orange-pulp,
With three sips the Arian frustrate
While he drains his at one gulp.

But, whatever your mood, you will generally find a rhyme to suit it. For English is rich in rhymes.

## METER

Meter comes from the Greek *metron* (measure) and is the measured rhythm of a line of verse. The simplest way to define a meter is to call it a series of lines of verse in which each line has the same number of strong beats—places where the voice of the reader stresses a word or a syllable of a word.

"Hickory dickory dock." As you read it, you say "HICKory DICKory DOCK." Your voice makes the stresses automatically. It is like a fist tapping a punching-bag three times. "HICK" and the bag flies away; "DICK" and you strike it as it returns; "DOCK" and the bag flies away for the last time. And when you read the next line, you do the same thing: "The MOUSE ran UP the CLOCK." Three more taps on the punching bag. Then, for variety's sake, the meter changes. "The CLOCK struck ONE, And DOWN he RUN." Only two taps apiece to the line this time. Then a return to the first three-tap meter: "HICKory DICKory DOCK."

The three-tap meter is called *trimeter* (three-foot),

the two-tap meter *dimeter* (two-foot). *Tetrameter* is four-foot meter, *pentameter* five-foot, and so on, from a meter as short as the *monometer* (one-foot) to the long *octometer* and *nonometer* (eight- and nine-foot). It is a wide range, a wide and varied keyboard.

The stressed and unstressed syllables in a poetic foot are rather like the dots and dashes in the Morse telegraphic code. In scanning poetry—that is, in analyzing it for its rhythm—they are usually represented by the following signs:

⌣ = dot = short syllable, unstressed by the voice

— = dash = long syllable, stressed by the voice

The syllables are not really long or short in themselves; it is the stress of the voice that counts. Feet are made up of combinations of stressed and unstressed syllables. Some of these combinations are:

——spondee

⌣—iambus ⌣⌣—anapest ⌣—⌣amphibrach

—⌣trochee —⌣⌣dactyl —⌣—amphimacer

Perhaps the easiest way to remember them is from this verse of Coleridge's:

Trochee trips from long to short;
From long to long in solemn sort
Slow Spondee stalks; strong foot! yet ill able
Ever to come up with dactyl trisyllable.
Iambics march from short to long—
With a leap and a bound the swift Anapests throng;
One syllable long, with one short at each side,
Amphibrachys hastes with a stately stride;—
First and last being long, middle short, Amphimacer
Strikes his thundering hoofs like a proud high-bred racer

Suppose we take two lines and scan them.

John Gilpin was a citizen
Of credit and reknown.

Read it and see where the strong stresses are.

> John GILpin WAS a CIT-i-ZEN
> Of CREDit AND reKNOWN

Then divide it into feet and mark the long and short syllables.

> John Gil | pin was | a cit | izen
> Of cred | it and | reknown.

The first line is iambic tetrameter, the second iambic trimeter. But listen to the beat of the anapests in

> I gal | loped, Dirck gal | loped, we gal | loped all three.

Here is tetrameter too, but a strongly anapestic tetrameter, making for a much longer line and a differing rhythm.

The great Greek meter was the *hexameter* (six-foot), the meter of the 'Iliad' and the 'Odyssey'. It has never acclimated itself very well in English, though we have an example in Longfellow's 'Evangeline':

> This is the | forest pri | meval, the | murmuring |
> pines and the | hemlocks.

The meter holding a similar position in English, the meter of Shakespeare's plays and Milton's 'Paradise Lost', is the iambic pentameter (short-long, five-foot meter). When it is unrhymed we give it a name of its own and call it *blank verse*. Here is Shakespeare.

> Once more unto the breach, dear friends, once more
> Or close the wall up with our English dead

and again

> The singing masons building roofs of gold

and again

> Tomorrow and tomorrow and tomorrow
> Creeps in this petty pace from day to day
> To the last syllable of recorded time;
> And all our yesterdays have lighted fools
> The way to dusty death. Out, out, brief candle!
> Life's but a walking shadow, a poor player
> That struts and frets his hour upon the stage
> And then is heard no more. . . .

Here is Milton.

> Of Man's first disobedience and the fruit
> Of that forbidden tree whose mortal taste
> Brought Death into the·world and all our woe . . .
> Sing, Heavenly Muse, . . .

and again

> Thick as autumnal leaves that strew the brooks
> Of Vallombrosa, . . .

Here is Robert Frost.

> Something there is that doesn't love a wall
> That sends the frozen ground-swell under it
> And spills the upper boulders in the sun.

All very different, all wonderfully varied, yet all using the same basic structure.

### PATTERN

There are certain set patterns in poetry as there are certain regular meters. For convenience in discussing rhyme schemes we indicate identical rhymes by the same letter. A *couplet* consists of two lines of verse rhyming *aa;* a *quatrain* of four lines, rhyming in various combinations. 'We'll go no more a roving' (quoted before) is a quatrain. The *heroic couplet* is two rhymed lines of verse in iambic pentameter. Alexander Pope, the waspish, superb technician who was one of the most characteristic poets of the Eighteenth Century, wrote largely in the heroic couplet and made it as trim and telling as the sting of a bee.

> A little learning is a dangerous thing.
> Drink deep, or taste not the Pierian spring.

The *Spenserian stanza* is named after Edmund Spenser, who wrote the 'Faerie Queene'. It is a form, often used to tell a story, in which each separate stanza consists of eight lines of iambic pentameter, rhyming *ababbcbc,* and a line of iambic hexameter at the end, rhyming *c.* This hexameter line is called an *Alexandrine.* The following example of a Spenserian stanza is from Lord Byron.

> Roll on, thou deep and dark blue Ocean—roll!
> Ten thousand fleets sweep over thee in vain;
> Man marks the earth with ruin—his control
> Stops with the shore;—upon the watery plain
> The wrecks are all thy deed, nor doth remain     .
> A shadow of man's ravage, save his own,
> When for a moment, like a drop of rain,
> He sinks into thy depths with bubbling groan,
> Without a grave, unknell'd, uncoffin'd and unknown!

Perhaps the most famous of the set patterns in English poetry is the *sonnet.* It must consist of fourteen lines of iambic pentameter, rhymed usually in one of two ways. Here is a sonnet on the sonnet itself, by Richard Watson Gilder.

> What is a sonnet? 'Tis the pearly shell
> That murmurs of the far-off murmuring sea;
> A precious jewel, carved most curiously;
> It is a little picture, painted well.

What is a sonnet? 'Tis the tear that fell
From a great poet's hidden ecstasy;
A two-edged sword, a star, a song—ah me!
Sometimes a heavy-tolling funeral bell.

This was the flame that shook with Dante's breath;
The solemn organ whereon Milton played
And the clear glass where Shakespeare's shadow falls;
A sea this is—beware who ventureth!
For like a fiord the narrow floor is laid
Mid-ocean deep sheer to the mountain-walls.

This sort of sonnet, rhyming *abbaabba cdecde,* we call a Petrarchan or Italian sonnet, from Petrarch, the great Italian poet. The other customary form of the sonnet, consisting of four quatrains with an ending couplet *(abab cdcd efef gg)*, we call a Shakespearean sonnet. Here is one of the great Shakespearean sonnets. Notice the difference in rhyme scheme.

Shall I compare thee to a Summer's day?
Thou art more lovely and more temperate:
Rough winds do shake the darling buds of May
And Summer's lease hath all too short a date.

Sometime too hot the eye of Heaven shines
And often is his gold complexion dimm'd;
And every fair from fair sometimes declines,
By chance, or nature's changing course, untrimm'd.

But thy eternal Summer shall not fade
Nor lose possession of that fair thou ow'st;
Nor shall Death brag thou wander'st in his shade,
When in eternal lines to time thou grow'st;

    So long as men can breathe, or eyes can see,
    So long lives this, and this gives life to thee.

The first eight lines of any sonnet are called the octave, the last six the sestet. The sonnet is a strict form; a poem with thirteen lines or fifteen lines,

though it may be a very beautiful poem, is not a son-
net. Gilder's own sonnet suggests some of the diffi-
culties facing the poet who wishes to bring his sonnet
to perfection.

Certain other forms, chiefly those borrowed from
the French (the *ballade, villanelle, rondeau,* and so
on), are also very strict patterns. That is the fun of
working in them—the fun of working within certain
known limits. Outside of these forms, the poet makes
his own pattern. He may write a poem as long as
'Paradise Lost' entirely in one meter, blank verse.
He may write as Shelley did in 'To A Skylark':

> Hail to thee, blithe spirit!
> Bird thou never wert,
> That from heaven, or near it,
> Pourest thy full heart
> In profuse strains of unpremeditated art.

Here the pattern in each stanza makes use of more
than one meter, more than one sort of rhyme, and
plays long lines against shorter ones. But once the
form is established, that form is followed throughout
the poem. The poet may write, as Matthew Arnold
does in the beginning of 'Philomela',

> Hark! ah, the nightingale!
> The tawny-throated!
> Hark! from that moonlit cedar what a burst!
> What triumph! hark, what pain!

Here the meter is irregular, the verse unrhymed;
it is the rhythmic pattern of the poem which makes
the music. In fact, once the poet knows his business,
he may do as he pleases, except in the strict forms.
He may write in free verse, blank verse, rhymed

verse, regular meters, irregular meters. But he must stir your imagination and do it in a way that is not the way of prose. If he writes

> At 10:35
> Mr. John W. Higgins
> Went down town to the grocery
> To get a loaf of bread,

he is not writing poetry but chopping up a piece of prose and arranging it in lines. If he writes, as Whitman did,

As toilsome I wandered Virginia's woods,
To the music of rustling leaves kicked up by my feet (for 'twas autumn)
I marked at the foot of a tree the grave of a soldier;
Mortally wounded he and buried on the retreat (easily all I could understand)
The halt of a mid-day hour when up! no time to lose—yet this sign left
On a tablet scrawled and nailed on the tree by the grave
*Bold, cautious, true and my loving comrade.*

Long, long I muse then on my way go wandering,
Many a changeful season to follow and many a scene of life
Yet at times through changeful season and scene, abrupt, alone or in the crowded street,
Comes before me the unknown soldier's grave, comes the inscription rude in Virginia's woods,
*Bold, cautious, true and my loving comrade.—*

he is writing poetry, though pattern and meter are irregular and there is no rhyme. But there is a music in the pattern, and the poem says more than its words. It is not told in the way of prose.

### THE VARIOUS KINDS OF POETRY

There are kinds of poetry as there are kinds of meters. A *lyric* is a brief, intense burst of music in words—"Where the bee sucks, there suck I"; "With rue my heart is laden"; "Come unto these yellow sands." It must mount into the air or it is nothing. A poem 250 lines long, though it might have lyric qualities, would not be a lyric. Lyric poetry is singing poetry.

*Elegiac* poetry grieves for a dead friend. Gray's 'Elegy in a Country Churchyard', Milton's 'Lycidas', and Tennyson's 'In Memoriam' are elegies. An *ode* usually deals with an exalted or impersonal subject in a somewhat formal pattern—Keats' 'Ode to a Grecian Urn' and Lowell's 'Commemoration Ode', though quite different in subject matter, are good examples of the form.

*Narrative* poetry tells a story. *Epic* poetry is, or should be, poetry dealing with heroic subjects in a heroic manner. A *ballad* is direct and simple, a swinging tune about war or love or stirring events—'The Bonny Earl of Murray' is a ballad. 'Casey Jones' is a folk-ballad of our own; so are such cowboy songs as 'The Old Chisholm Trail'.

*Dramatic* poetry builds a drama or play. Shakespeare's plays are the best examples of dramatic poetry in English. *Didactic* poetry is intended to teach a lesson or to point a moral. Pope's 'Essay on Criticism' is of this type.

## HOW TO LEARN TO APPRECIATE POETRY

The poems we first hear in childhood—the nursery rhymes, the verses in first readers—are usually rhymed poems with a strong, simple beat. Later on we come to poetry that is unrhymed and sometimes, in modern poetry, to poetry that seems at first glance to lack both rhyme and pattern. How can we appreciate this? We must train our ear for it, as we train our ear in music to appreciate counterpoint and harmony. We can do so best by remembering first of all that poetry is meant to be heard as well as read. If a passage or a poem seems unmelodious to you at first, read it over to yourself, aloud or half-aloud, feeling for the music and the pattern that were in the poet's mind.

If in classic poetry you encounter such queer creatures as Arimaspians, such allusions as "Thee bright-haired Vesta long of yore To solitary Saturn bore," such words and contractions of words as *eftsoons, prithee, 'twas,* and *erst,*—find out what they mean, of course, but get the rhythm of the music first. You need not know, for instance, in the lines of Milton's quoted previously, the exact geography of Vallom-brosa; the rustling word itself tells you that it is a place where leaves fall thickly in the autumn. You need not know, at first glance, all the technical merits and defects of a poem, any more than you have to know about all the nails in a chair to like the chair. It is a good thing to stretch your mind against the close-packed thought of certain great passages of poetry, but first of all let the words sing to you. If, in modern poetry, certain words and phrases seem to you "unpoetic," remember that poetry is made from live words, current words, not dead ones. It must have the salt and sting of life in it, or it is not great. And remember also that as a modern poet, Archibald Mac-Leish, has said,

It is true also that we here are Americans:
That we use the machines: that a sight of the god is
  unusual . . .

The things of the poet are done to a man alone.

Each age makes its own poetry. It cannot copy the poetry of a past age and produce living work. And poetry is not all in books; some of it is being made today. Only, it must be heard.

## THE MAGIC AND MYSTERY OF POETRY

For that is the first thing poetry asks—to be heard. After that there are other things. There is the curiously magical effect of certain words, certain sounds, certain images brought together. "Come unto these yellow sands And then take hands." "Old unhappy far-off things And battles long ago." "O, we were sisters, sisters seven! We were the fairest under heaven!" There are lines that stir the mind like a bugle, and lines that fade away into forest-distances, "Annihilating all that's made To a green thought in a green shade." There are lines that seem to hold great wisdom and great peace: "I saw Eternity the other night Like a great ring of pure and endless light All calm as it was bright." But they must be heard before they become part of our minds.

The poet William Blake once wrote: " 'What?' it will be questioned, 'When the Sun rises, do you not see a round disk of fire somewhat like a guinea?' O no, no, I see an innumerable company of the heavenly Host, crying 'Holy, Holy, Holy is the Lord God Almighty!' I question not my corporal or vegetative eye any more than I would question a window, concerning a sight. I look through it and not with it."

The difference between those two ways of looking at the sun is the difference between the prose way of looking at life and the poetic way. Not because poetry asks us to live in an unreal world; that is not its purpose. But it can make the world we live in different and more shining.

# STEPHEN VINCENT BENÉT

*By* Mabel Scacheri

THE strange story of America has slipped like quicksilver through the fingers of many writers. Pirates in white-sailed ships, adventurers in bright armor, plumed and painted Indians, gnarled pioneers with restless feet, the great green wilderness, shattering new thoughts and ways, bitter wars, gleaming machines shaking the world from end to end—all these are strands in the great American story.

Out of it have come huge gusts of bombast, synthetic nonsense about cowboys and Indians, false patriotic jingles. Yet America, though inured to the tinny sound of quick and easy harpings on the American theme, knew at once when its own song was sung by Stephen Vincent Benét. The awards of the Pulitzer prize (1929) and the Theodore Roosevelt medal (1933) were merely confirmation of the stirred feelings of the general public.

Naturally it was no accident that the poet Stephen Vincent Benét became one of the authentic voices of the American spirit. Benét came of a stock rooted for generations in America. As a boy he moved from one side of the continent to the other, and felt its vastness and variety. He was born in Bethlehem, Pa., on July 22, 1898. His father, grandfather, and great-grandfather had been army officers, and his grandfather had written books on military subjects. When Stephen was seven, his family moved from New York to California, his father having been transferred to Benicia arsenal.

STEPHEN VINCENT BENÉT

There were other moves. The boy went to school in California and in Georgia.

Benét's talent developed early. The literary world was surprised in 1915 by the publication of a set of dramatic monologs, 'Five Men and Pompey'. The author was then seventeen.

He was graduated from Yale in 1919, and went to the Sorbonne to study. In Paris he met Rosemary Carr of Chicago, then on the staff of the Paris edition of the *Chicago Tribune*. They were later married in Chicago.

For some years he wrote novels and short stories. His poem "King David" won *The Nation's* poetry prize in 1923. 'John Brown's Body', published in 1928, was written during two years spent at Neuilly, France, on a Guggenheim fellowship.

The Benéts now live in New York City, with their three children, Stephanie Jane, Thomas Carr, and Rachel. Stephen is the younger brother of William Rose Benét and Laura Benét, who are also poets of distinction. The name is pronounced Be-NAY, and is of Spanish origin.

In temperament Benét is quiet and humorous, a good talker among a few people, and a gifted demolisher of cherished prejudices. As a poet he excels in the ballad style, in drumming out magnificent stanzas, in shifting from meter to meter, in setting in motion a living pageant of legend and history.

His feeling for the magic of America is breath-taking. We come upon this in 'A Book of Americans', a volume of verses for children:

When Daniel Boone goes by, at night,
The phantom deer arise
And all lost, wild America
Is burning in their eyes.

Quick and telling images light up picture after picture: A nurse "stayed as white and silent as an egg"—"A laugh like a double-barrelled gun"—"the nun-footed night"—"the war-painted dawns" of the west—oxen's noses "black and wet as snailshells"—"I only bring a cup of silver air."

Years of study in Paris have not persuaded him to exchange his birthright for a few genteel villanelles about the lights reflected in the Seine. He tells us:

I have fallen in love with American names,
The sharp names that never get fat,
The snakeskin-titles of mining-claims,
The plumed war-bonnet of Medicine Hat,
Tucson and Deadwood and Lost Mule Flat.

Keenly he senses the roots of the present in the past:

Out of John Brown's strong sinews the tall skyscrapers grow.

Stephen Vincent Benét is one of the most vital of modern American poets.

His published poetical works are 'Five Men and Pompey', 1915; 'Young Adventure', 1918; 'Heavens and Earth', 1920; 'Ballad of William Sycamore', 1923; 'Tiger Joy', 1925; 'John Brown's Body', 1928; 'Ballads and Poems', 1931; and, with his wife Rosemary, 'A Book of Americans', 1933. His novels are 'The Beginning of Wisdom', 1921; 'Young People's Pride', 1922; 'Jean Huguenot', 1923; 'Spanish Bayonet', 1926; 'James Shore's Daughter', 1934.

A new collection of verse, 'The Burning City', will be published in 1936.